Introduction

In a world where people constantly feel judged, betrayed, alone, and misunderstood, it can be challenging to stay true to oneself while maintaining healthy relationships. This book is designed to help you establish and enforce boundaries in a way that aligns with your faith and deepens your walk with Christ.

Through multiple affirmations, prayers, and reflection challenges, I Know Who I Am will guide you in defining personal limits that protect your peace, strengthen your identity in Christ, and promote healthier relationships. Each section is tailored to specific struggles—whether it's setting boundaries in friendships, navigating marriage, handling betrayal, or managing expectations in motherhood.

You are called to walk in truth, love, and wisdom. May this book be a tool to help you confidently declare: I know who I am in Christ, and I will honor the life He has called me to live.

Table of Contents

I Know Who I Am:
A Bible-Based Affirmations and Reflections Guide

- **UNDERSTANDING BOUNDARIES FROM A BIBLICAL PERSPECTIVE**
- **AFFIRMATIONS & REFLECTIONS BY CATEGORY:**
  - **FRIENDSHIPS**
  - **LOVE RELATIONSHIPS & MARRIAGE**
  - **MOTHERHOOD**
  - **DEALING WITH BETRAYAL**
  - **WORKPLACE & PROFESSIONAL BOUNDARIES**
  - **FAMILY & RELATIONAL EXPECTATIONS**
  - **SPIRITUAL GROWTH & PERSONAL CONVICTIONS**
- **PRACTICAL CHALLENGES TO STRENGTHEN BOUNDARIES**
- **CLOSING PRAYER & ENCOURAGEMENT**

Understanding Boundaries from a Biblical Perspective

Boundaries are not just a modern concept—they are deeply rooted in biblical wisdom. Throughout Scripture, God demonstrates the importance of setting healthy boundaries for protection, clarity, and spiritual growth. Just as He established physical and spiritual boundaries for His people, we are also called to define limits that align with His truth.

Why Are Boundaries Important?
- **They reflect God's design.** In creation, God set boundaries for the land, sea, and sky (Genesis 1:9-10). Just as He established order in the world, we must establish order in our lives.
- **They protect our hearts.** Proverbs 4:23 reminds us, "Guard your heart above all else, for it determines the course of your life." Setting boundaries helps us safeguard our emotional, mental, and spiritual well-being.
- **Jesus modeled boundaries.** Christ loved and served others, yet He also withdrew to pray (Luke 5:16), set limits on His time (Mark 1:35-38), and was clear about His mission (John 6:15).
- **They allow us to love others better.** Healthy boundaries prevent resentment, burnout, and unhealthy relationships, allowing us to give and receive love as God intended (Matthew 22:39).

How Do We Set God-Honoring Boundaries?
1. **Recognize your worth in Christ**. Knowing who you are in Him gives you the confidence to set limits without guilt.
2. **Seek wisdom through Scripture.** The Bible provides clear guidance on healthy relationships, priorities, and discernment.
3. **Pray for strength and clarity**. Asking God for wisdom (James 1:5) ensures that your boundaries reflect His will.
4. **Communicate with love and grace.** Boundaries should be set with a spirit of kindness, not defensiveness or fear.
5. **Stay firm but flexible.** While boundaries are essential, they should be guided by the Holy Spirit and adjusted when necessary.

By understanding boundaries from a biblical perspective, you will not only protect your peace but also walk in the freedom and confidence of your God-given identity.

Friendships

SCRIPTURE

- **1 Corinthians 15:33 (NIV)** – "Do not be misled: 'Bad company corrupts good character.'"
- **2 Corinthians 6:14 (NIV)** – "Do not be yoked together with unbelievers. For what do righteousness and wickedness have in common? Or what fellowship can light have with darkness?"
- **Romans 12:2 (NIV)** – "Do not conform to the pattern of this world, but be transformed by the renewing of your mind. Then you will be able to test and approve what God's will is—his good, pleasing and perfect will."
- **Proverbs 13:20 (NIV)** – "Walk with the wise and become wise, for a companion of fools suffers harm."
- **James 4:4 (NIV)** – "You adulterous people, don't you know that friendship with the world means enmity against God? Therefore, anyone who chooses to be a friend of the world becomes an enemy of God."

PRAYER

LORD, GUIDE ME IN CHOOSING FRIENDS WHO UPLIFT AND SUPPORT MY WALK WITH YOU. HELP ME TO RECOGNIZE RELATIONSHIPS THAT DRAIN MY SPIRIT AND GIVE ME THE STRENGTH TO SET FIRM BUT LOVING BOUNDARIES.

Reflection Challenge

Think of a time when a friend crossed your boundaries. How did you handle it? What would you do differently now?

....
....
....
....
....
....
....
....
....
....
....
....
....
....
....
....
....
....
....
....
....
....

Love & Marriage

AFFIRMATION

I WILL HONOR GOD IN MY

RELATIONSHIPS BY

ESTABLISHING CLEAR,

RESPECTFUL BOUNDARIES.

AFFIRMATION

GOD'S LOVE IS MY

FOUNDATION; I WILL NOT

SETTLE FOR LESS THAN HIS

BEST FOR ME.

SCRIPTURE

- **Proverbs 4:23 (NIV)** – "Above all else, guard your heart, for everything you do flows from it."
- **Ephesians 5:25 (NIV)** – "Husbands, love your wives, just as Christ loved the church and gave himself up for her."
- **Ecclesiastes 4:9-10 (NIV)** – "Two are better than one, because they have a good return for their labor: If either of them falls down, one can help the other up. But pity anyone who falls and has no one to help them up."
- **1 Corinthians 13:4-7 (NIV)** – "Love is patient, love is kind. It does not envy, it does not boast, it is not proud. It does not dishonor others, it is not self-seeking, it is not easily angered, it keeps no record of wrongs. Love does not delight in evil but rejoices with the truth. It always protects, always trusts, always hopes, always perseveres."
- **Matthew 7:24-25 (NIV)** – "Therefore everyone who hears these words of mine and puts them into practice is like a wise man who built his house on the rock. The rain came down, the streams rose, and the winds blew and beat against that house; yet it did not fall, because it had its foundation on the rock."

PRAYER

FATHER, GIVE ME WISDOM IN MY RELATIONSHIPS. LET MY LOVE BE PATIENT AND KIND, YET FIRM IN HONORING MY PERSONAL AND SPIRITUAL VALUES.

Reflection Challenge

Identify one area in your relationship where you've compromised your values. What steps can you take to realign your relationship with God's principles?

....

....

....

....

....

....

....

....

....

....

....

....

....

....

....

....

....

....

....

....

Motherhood

SCRIPTURE

- *"Train up a child in the way he should go; even when he is old he will not depart from it." - Proverbs 22:6*
- *"She is clothed with strength and dignity; she can laugh at the days to come." - Proverbs 31:25*
- *"Behold, children are a heritage from the Lord, the fruit of the womb a reward." - Psalm 127:3*
- *"A wise woman builds her home, but a foolish woman tears it down with her own hands." - Proverbs 14:1*
- *"I have no greater joy than to hear that my children are walking in the truth." - 3 John 1:4*

PRAYER

LORD, HELP ME LEAD MY CHILDREN WITH GRACE AND DISCIPLINE. TEACH ME TO BALANCE LOVE AND CORRECTION WHILE PROTECTING MY PEACE.

Reflection Challenge

Reflect on an area in your parenting where boundaries need to be reinforced. How can you approach this in a Christ-centered way?

....

....

....

....

....

....

....

....

....

....

....

....

....

....

....

....

....

....

....

....

....

Dealing with Betrayal

AFFIRMATION

I WILL NOT ALLOW BETRAYAL
TO DEFINE ME. MY WORTH IS
ROOTED IN CHRIST, NOT IN
OTHERS' ACTIONS.

AFFIRMATION

I CHOOSE FORGIVENESS, BUT
I WILL ALSO PROTECT MY
HEART WITH WISDOM.

SCRIPTURE

- *"The Lord is close to the brokenhearted and saves those who are crushed in spirit." - Psalm 34:18*
- *"Bless those who persecute you; bless and do not curse." - Romans 12:14*
- *"But I say to you, Love your enemies and pray for those who persecute you." - Matthew 5:44*
- *"Do not repay evil with evil or insult with insult. On the contrary, repay evil with blessing." - 1 Peter 3:9*
- *"Even my close friend, someone I trusted, one who shared my bread, has turned against me." - Psalm 41:9*

PRAYER

JESUS, YOU WERE BETRAYED, YET YOU CHOSE FORGIVENESS. HELP ME
RELEASE ANGER AND PAIN WHILE MAINTAINING NECESSARY BOUNDARIES
TO PROTECT MY HEART.

Reflection Challenge

Write a letter to someone who has betrayed you—express your feelings honestly, but from a place of healing. You don't need to send it; this is for your own closure.

....
....
....
....
....
....
....
....
....
....
....
....
....
....
....
....
....
....
....
....
....

Workplace / Professional

AFFIRMATION	AFFIRMATION
I WILL NOT OVEREXTEND MYSELF AT THE EXPENSE OF MY PEACE AND WELL-BEING.	MY WORK IS UNTO THE LORD, AND I WILL SET BOUNDARIES THAT HONOR HIM.

SCRIPTURE

- *"Whatever you do, work at it with all your heart, as working for the Lord, not for human masters." - Colossians 3:23*
- *"Do not be slothful in zeal, be fervent in spirit, serve the Lord." - Romans 12:11*
- *"A false balance is an abomination to the Lord, but a just weight is his delight." - Proverbs 11:1*
- *"Do not be unequally yoked with unbelievers." - 2 Corinthians 6:14*
- *"The plans of the diligent lead to profit as surely as haste leads to poverty." - Proverbs 21:5*

PRAYER

LORD, HELP ME NAVIGATE MY WORK WITH INTEGRITY AND BALANCE. SHOW ME HOW TO STAND FIRM IN MY VALUES WHILE EXCELLING IN MY CAREER.

Reflection Challenge

Assess your work-life balance. What changes can you make to set more clear boundaries?

....
....
....
....
....
....
....
....
....
....

....
....
....
....
....
....
....
....
....
....

Family Expectations

SCRIPTURE

- *"Honor your father and mother." - Exodus 20:12*
- *"If possible, so far as it depends on you, live peaceably with all."- Romans 12:18*
- *"Do to others as you would have them do to you." - Luke 6:31*
- *"A friend loves at all times, and a brother is born for adversity." - Proverbs 17:17*
- *"Bear with each other and forgive one another if any of you has a grievance." - Colossians 3:13*

PRAYER

FATHER, GIVE ME THE COURAGE TO SET BOUNDARIES WITH FAMILY WITHOUT FEAR OF REJECTION. LET MY LOVE BE FIRM AND UNWAVERING IN TRUTH.

Reflection Challenge

Identify a situation where you've struggled with family boundaries. What is one action step you can take to improve it?

....
....
....
....
....
....
....
....
....
....
....
....
....
....
....
....
....
....
....
....
....
....
....
....
....
....

Spiritual Growth

AFFIRMATION	**AFFIRMATION**
I WILL PRIORITIZE MY SPIRITUAL GROWTH AND NOT ALLOW DISTRACTIONS TO PULL ME AWAY FROM MY PURPOSE.	MY IDENTITY IS FOUND IN CHRIST, NOT IN THE OPINIONS OF OTHERS.

SCRIPTURE

- *Do not conform to the pattern of this world, but be transformed by the renewing of your mind. Then you will be able to test and approve what God's will is—his good, pleasing and perfect will." - Romans 12:2*
- *"But seek first his kingdom and his righteousness, and all these things will be given to you as well." - Matthew 6:33*
- *"I press on toward the goal to win the prize for which God has called me heavenward in Christ Jesus." - Philippians 3:14*
- *"His divine power has given us everything we need for a godly life through our knowledge of him who called us by his own glory and goodness." - 2 Peter 1:3*
- *"How can a young person stay on the path of purity? By living according to your word." - Psalm 119:9*

PRAYER

LORD, HELP ME TO STAY STEADFAST IN MY FAITH. GIVE ME THE DISCERNMENT TO WALK AWAY FROM ANYTHING THAT HINDERS MY GROWTH IN YOU.

Reflection Challenge

Set a goal for your spiritual growth—whether it's daily prayer, Bible study, or joining a faith-based group. How will you commit to it?

....

....

....

....

....

....

....

....

....

....

....

....

....

....

....

....

....

....

....

....

....

....

....

....

PRACTICAL CHALLENGES TO STRENGTHEN BOUNDARIES

Setting and maintaining boundaries is not just about recognizing where limits should be placed, but about having the courage and discipline to uphold them. Below are general and category-specific challenges designed to help you apply what you've learned:

Identify Your Core Values – Write down five non-negotiable values that you refuse to compromise in any relationship. These will serve as the foundation for your boundaries.

Practice Saying No – For the next week, intentionally say no to one request that violates your boundaries, even if it's uncomfortable.

Set a Time Limit – If certain people drain your energy or pull you into unhealthy patterns, limit the time you spend with them. Set a maximum time for calls, visits, or engagements.

Pray for Discernment – Ask God daily for wisdom in distinguishing relationships that need stronger boundaries and those that need nurturing.

Accountability Check – Ask a trusted mentor or friend to hold you accountable for keeping your boundaries firm.

Friendships: Evaluate your circle and identify one relationship that has negatively impacted your faith or well-being. Decide on an action step—whether it's a conversation, distancing, or complete separation.

Love Relationships & Marriage: Write a prayer for your current or future spouse, asking God to align your relationship with His purpose and to give you strength in setting and maintaining healthy boundaries.

Family & Relational Expectations:
Choose a family-related boundary that needs reinforcement (e.g., personal space, decision-making). Clearly communicate this boundary to the appropriate person.

Motherhood:
Establish a self-care boundary this week. Whether it's taking quiet time for prayer, rest, or a personal activity, commit to it and do not let guilt override your need for balance.

Dealing with Betrayal:
Reflect on past betrayals and write a letter of forgiveness—not to send, but to release any lingering bitterness and affirm your commitment to healthy boundaries in future relationships.

Workplace & Professional Boundaries:
Set a firm boundary at work, such as leaving on time, not engaging in gossip, or not taking on extra work that is beyond your responsibilities.

Spiritual Growth & Personal Convictions:
Choose one spiritual practice (e.g., morning devotion, fasting, or worship time) and establish a firm boundary around it. Let nothing interfere with this commitment for the next seven days.

By consistently implementing these challenges, you will develop the strength and confidence needed to maintain boundaries that align with your faith and values.

Closing Prayer

Heavenly Father,
Thank You for guiding me through this journey of self-discovery, faith, and boundaries. I am grateful for the wisdom You have provided through Your Word, reminding me of who I am in Christ. Lord, help me to stand firm in my identity, to uphold the boundaries that protect my heart, and to walk in love without compromising the truth You have placed within me.

Give me discernment in my relationships, strength in my convictions, and peace in my decisions. When I feel weak, remind me that Your grace is sufficient. When I feel alone, remind me that You are always with me. And when I struggle to enforce my boundaries, remind me that obedience to You is greater than the approval of man.

May my life reflect Your love and wisdom as I continue to grow in faith. Let my boundaries not be walls that shut others out, but gates that allow only what is good, holy, and aligned with Your purpose. I surrender all to You, trusting that as I set my boundaries, You will protect, restore, and bless my path.

In Jesus' name, I pray, Amen.

Try Another Challenge!

7-DAY HEALING FOR THE BETRAYED

"A short but powerful journey for the betrayed seeking healing, clarity, and renewal.

OVERCOMING DEPRESSION

Explore the root causes of depression and get faith-based solutions, scripture breakdowns, and practical steps for healing, renewal, and lasting transformation..

COURAGE TO COMMIT

This 30-day challenge will challenge your heart, renew your mind, and position you to walk boldly in your faith. If you've ever felt stuck in cycles of doubt, compromise, or lukewarm faith, this is your opportunity to break free and fully commit to God.

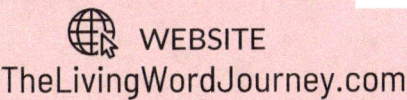

WEBSITE
TheLivingWordJourney.com

www.ingramcontent.com/pod-product-compliance
Lightning Source LLC
Chambersburg PA
CBHW071547120626
46550CB00006B/2617